Fantastic Creatures

by
Tabz Jones

Books by Tabz Jones

Digital Landscape Adult Coloring Book

Fantasy Art Mini Adult Coloring Book

Sun and Sand Adult Coloring Book

Gothic Fairy Dream Journal

Rockabilly Roses Journal

Dark Matter Adult Coloring Book

Gothic Girls Adult Coloring Book Volumes 1-7

Dangerous Curves Adult Coloring Book

Fantasy Men Adult Coloring Book

Harlequinn Pastel Fantasy Dream Journal

Gothiscopic Kaleidoscopes Coloring Book

Darling Dolls

Fantastic Creatures

Gothic Girls Art Book

Rose Cross Dream Journal

Reflections Vampire Poetry

Steampunk Adult Coloring Book

Angelic Book of Shadows

Fantasy Fae Adult Coloring Book

Fractal Art Adult Coloring Book Volumes 1-2

In Loving Memory Churchyard Adult Coloring Book

Fantasy Art Adult Coloring Book Volumes 1-2

Doodle Monsters Adult Coloring Book

Summer Flowers Adult Coloring Book

Skullz Adult Coloring Book Volumes 1-2

Dark Fantasy Adult Coloring Book Volumes 1-3

Classic Swears Adult Coloring Book Standard and Mini Editions

Statuesque Adult Coloring Book

ISBN-13: 978-1535580168

ISBN-10: 153558016X

Tabz Jones

PO BOX 2137

Alma AR 72921

www.gothictoggs.net

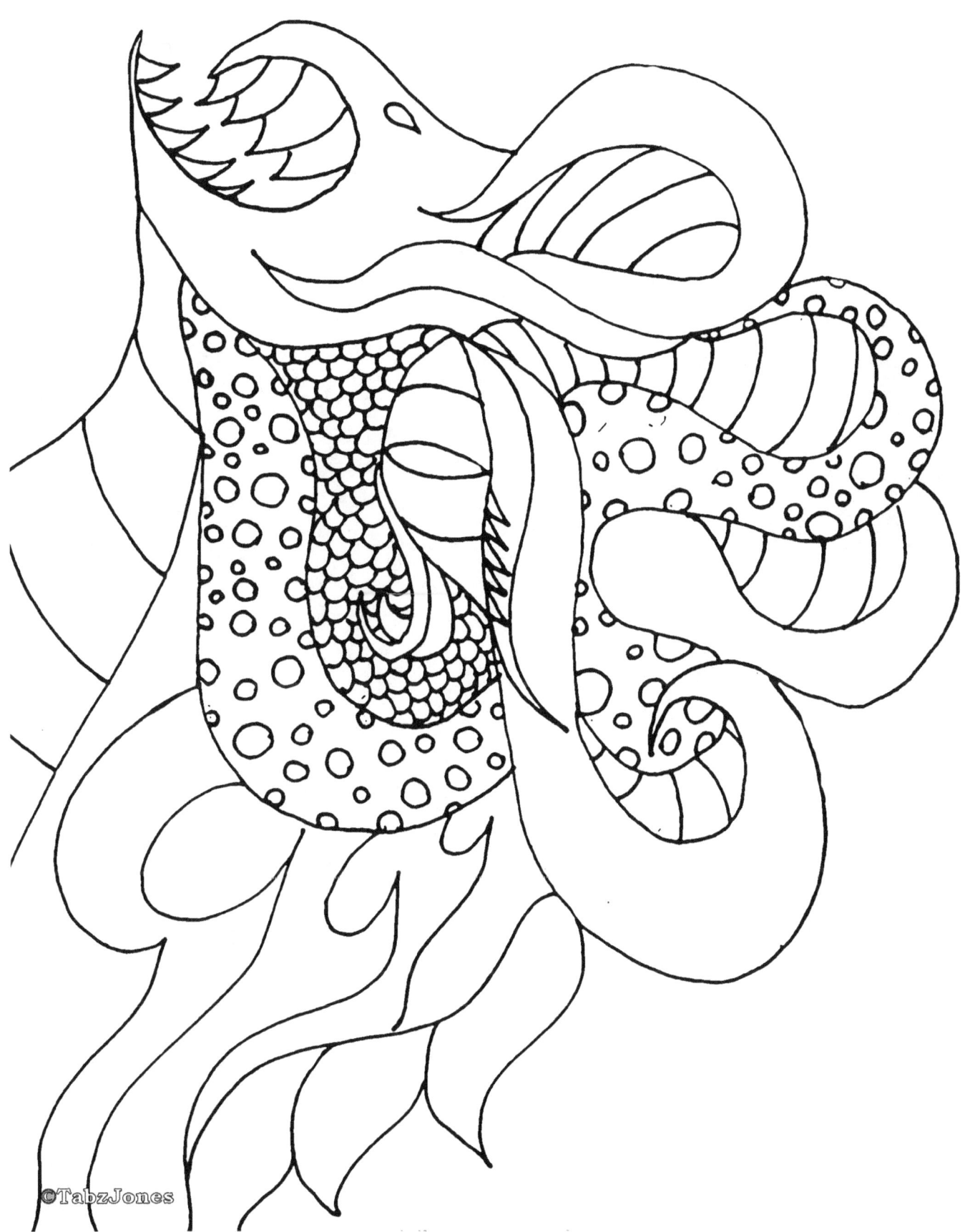

©TabzJones

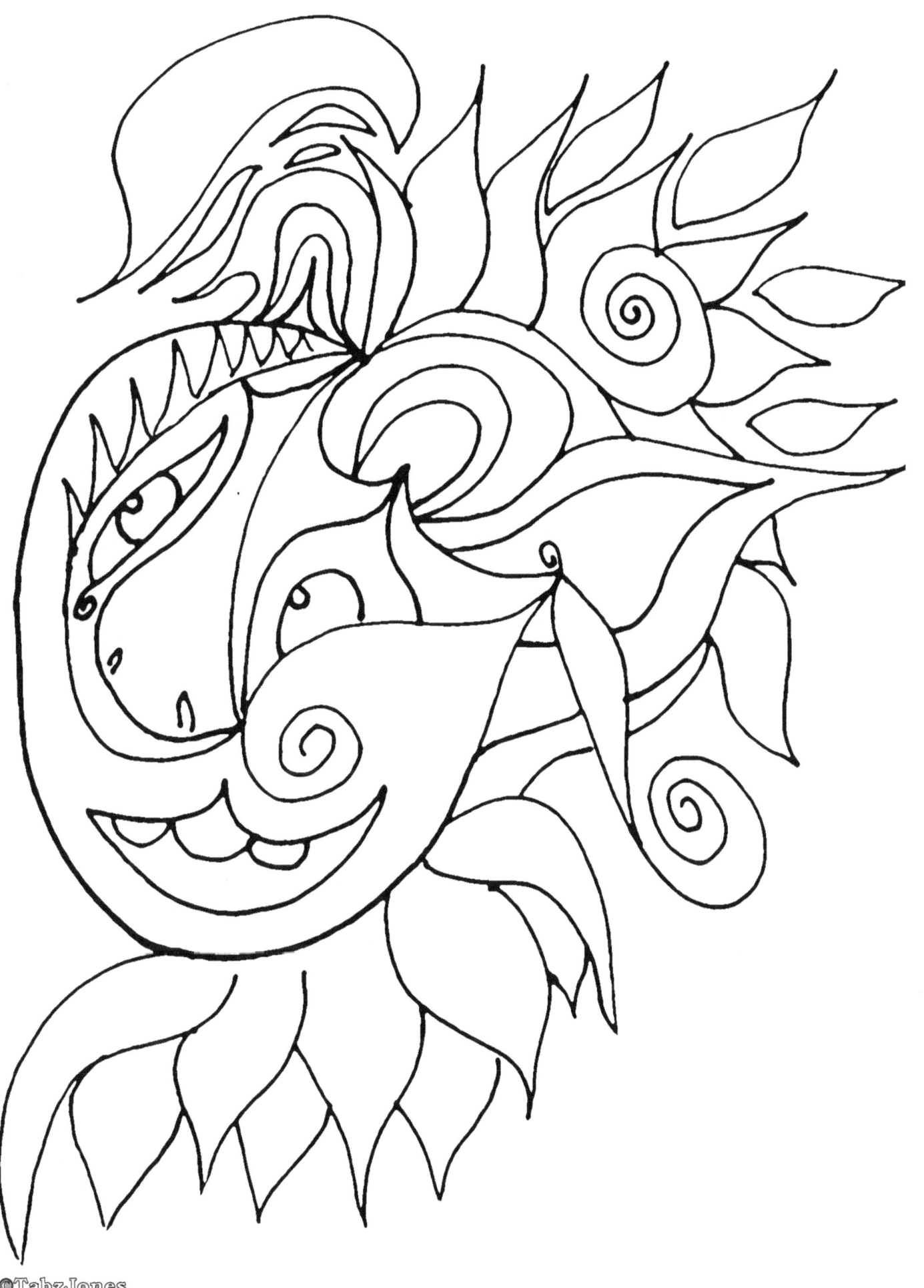

©TabzJones

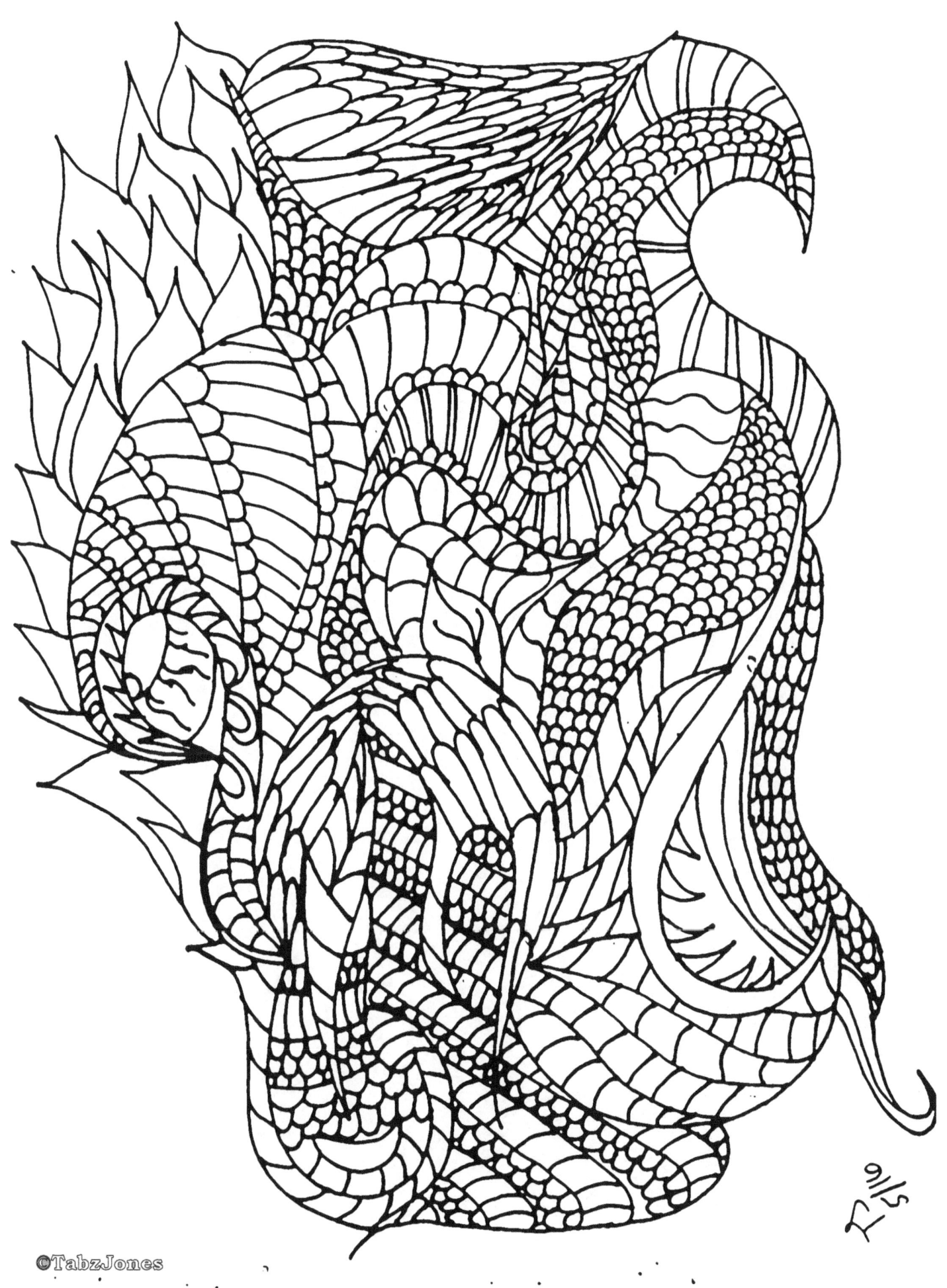

©TabzJones

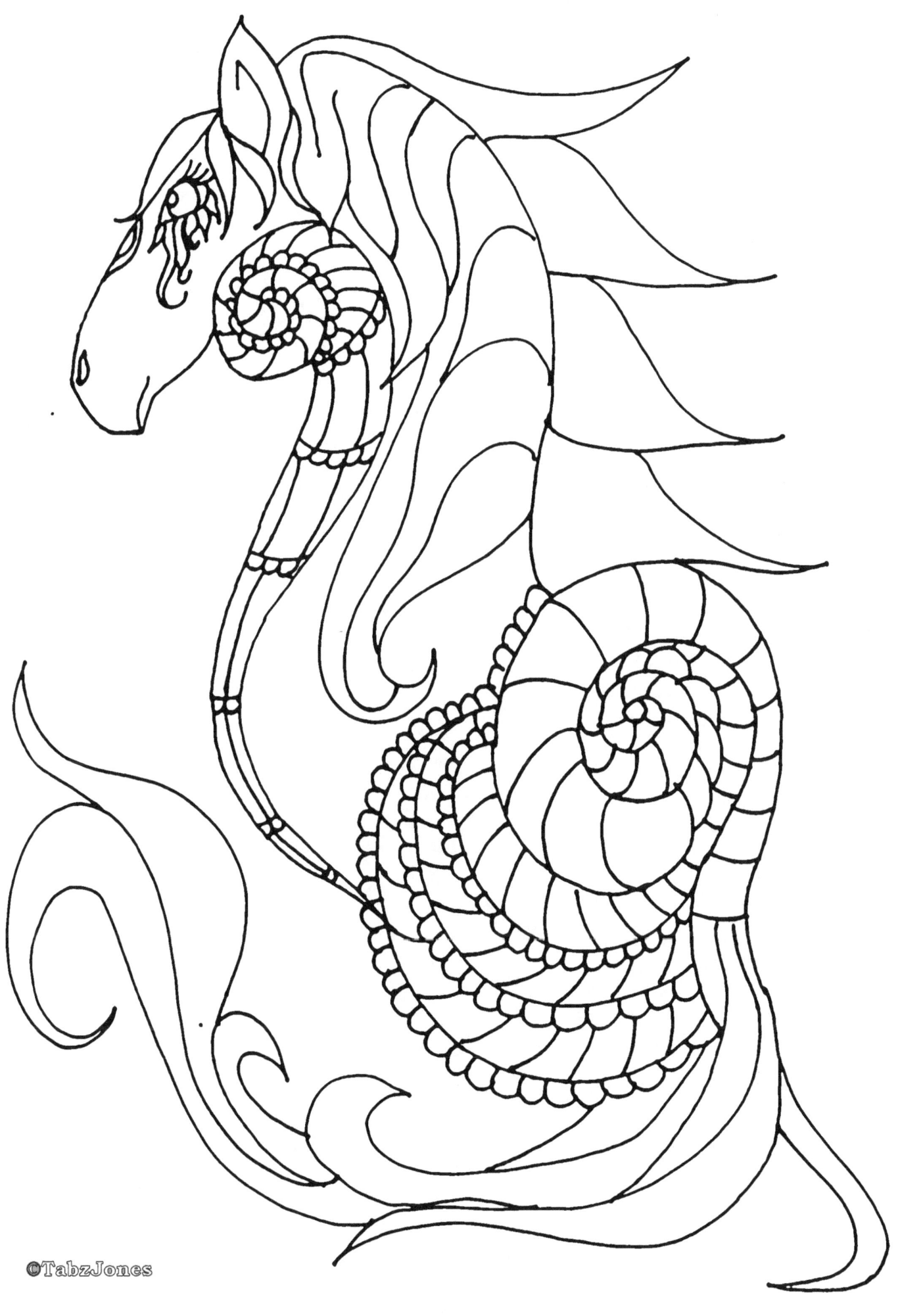

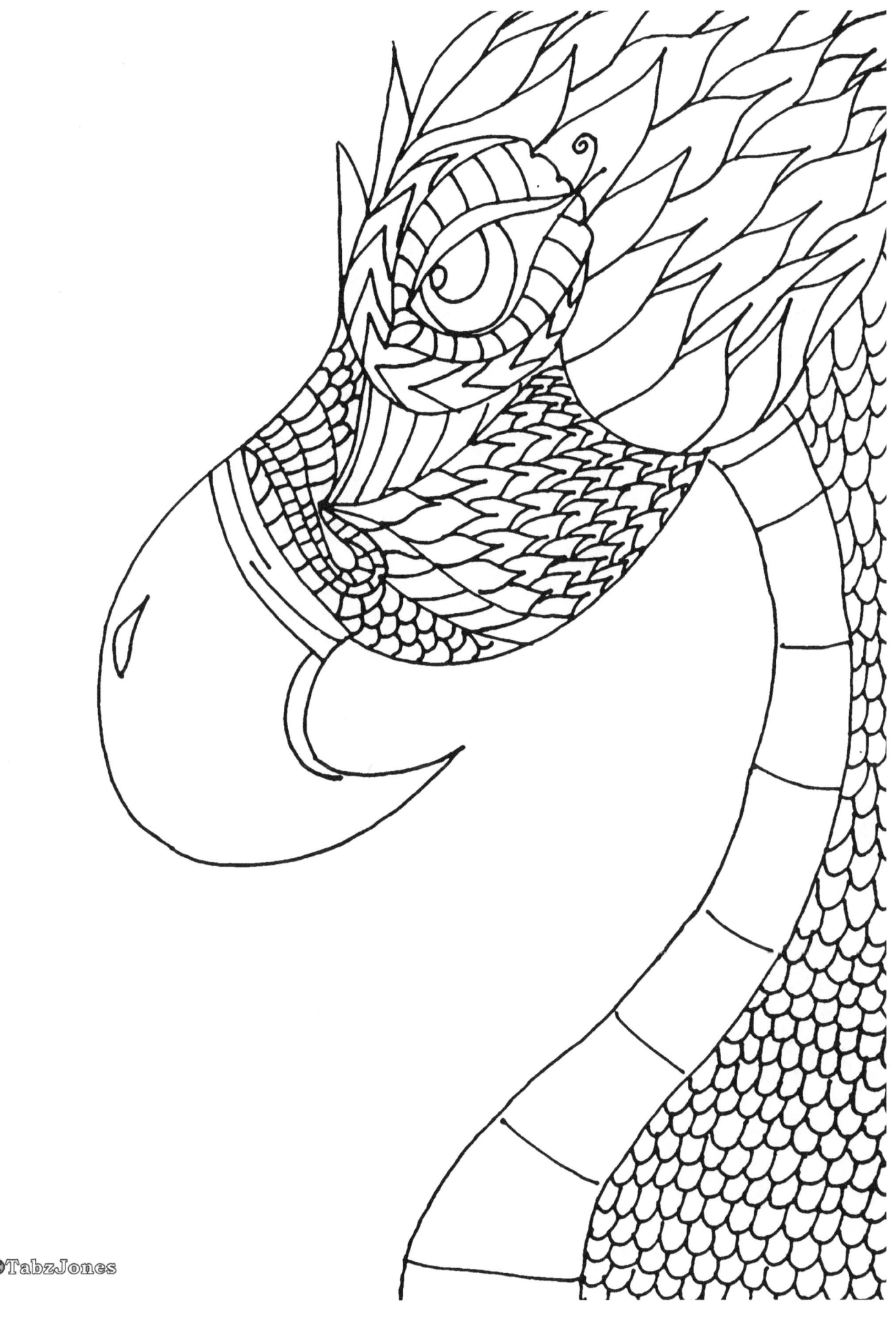

©TabzJones

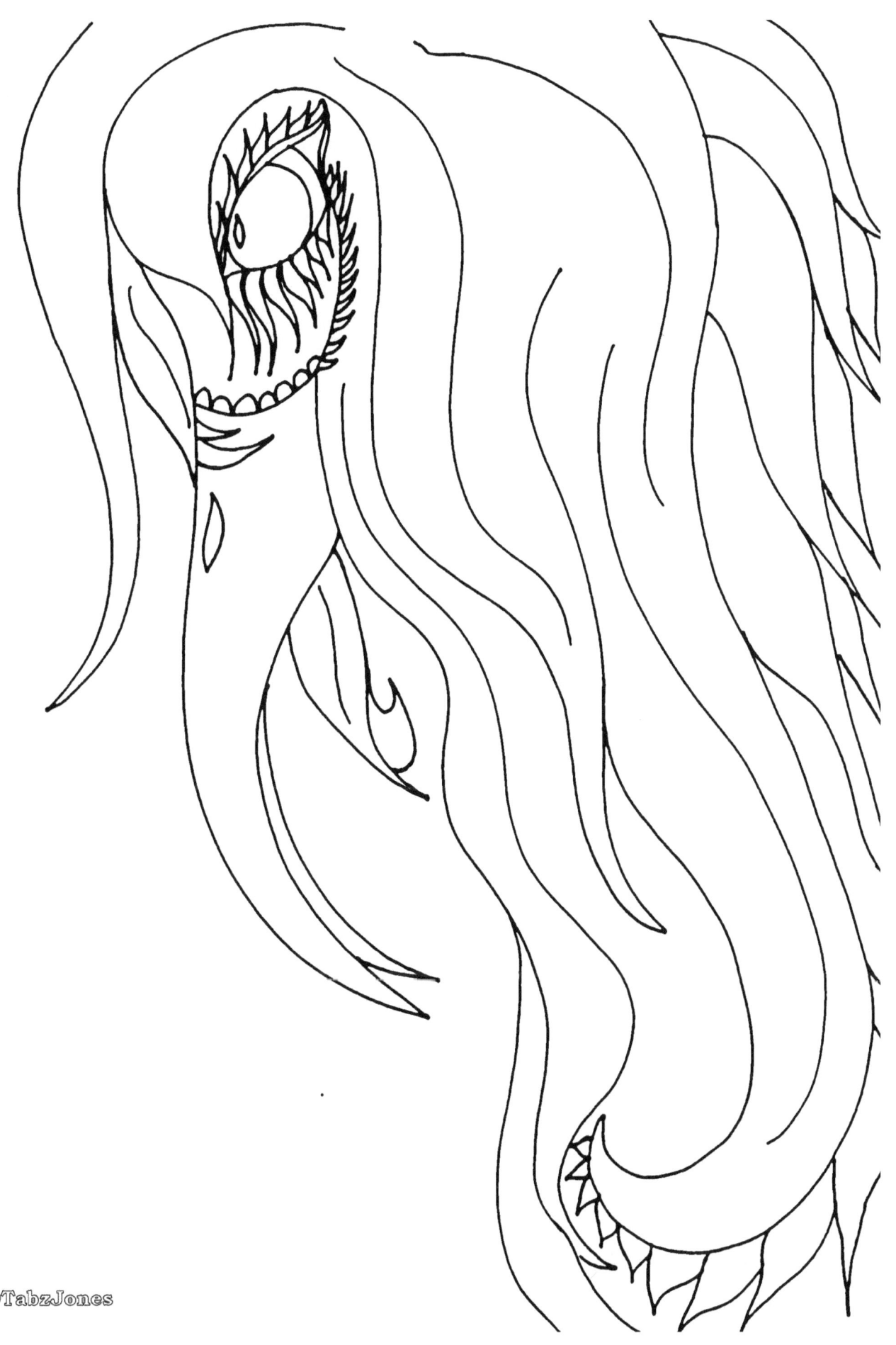

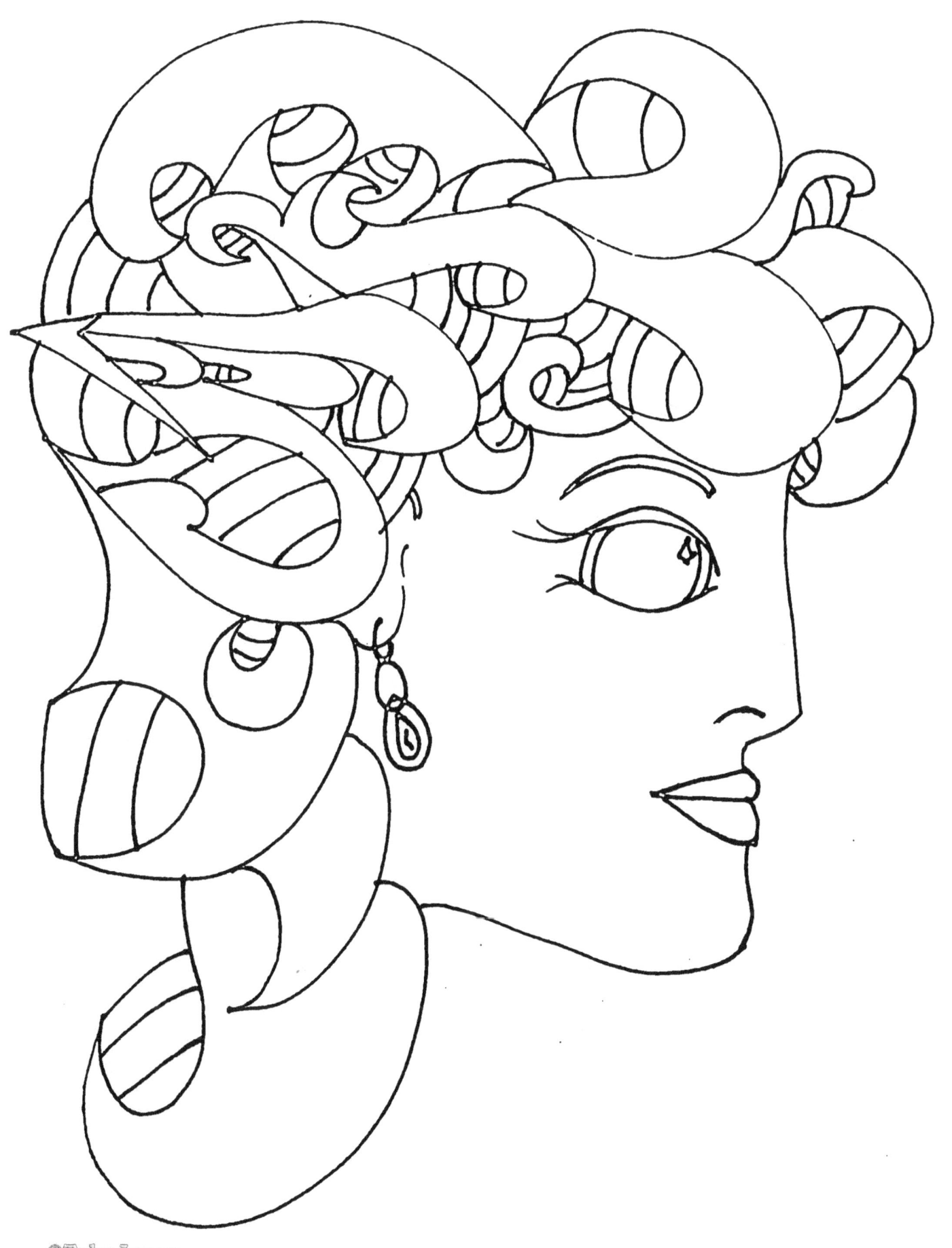

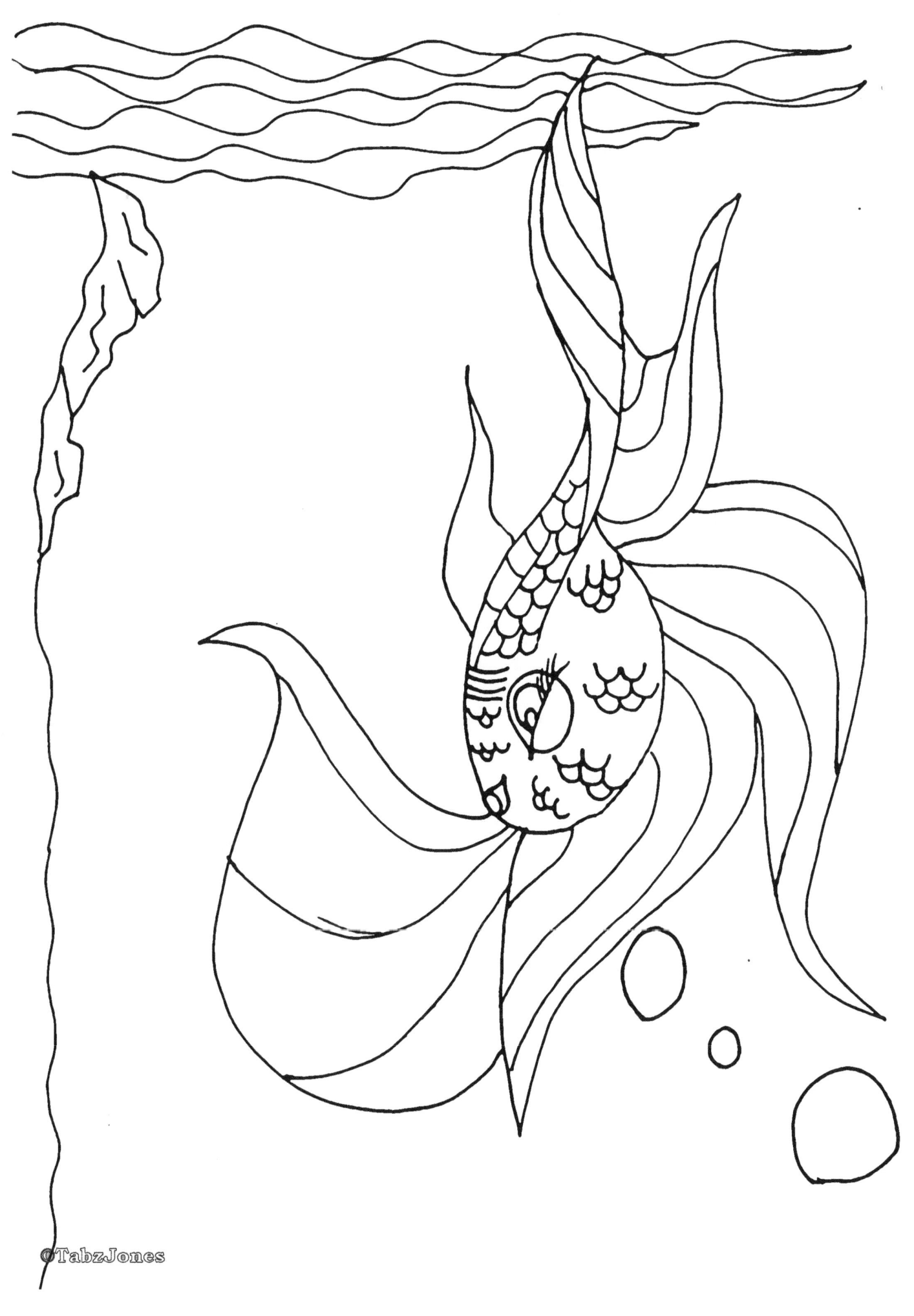

©TabzJones

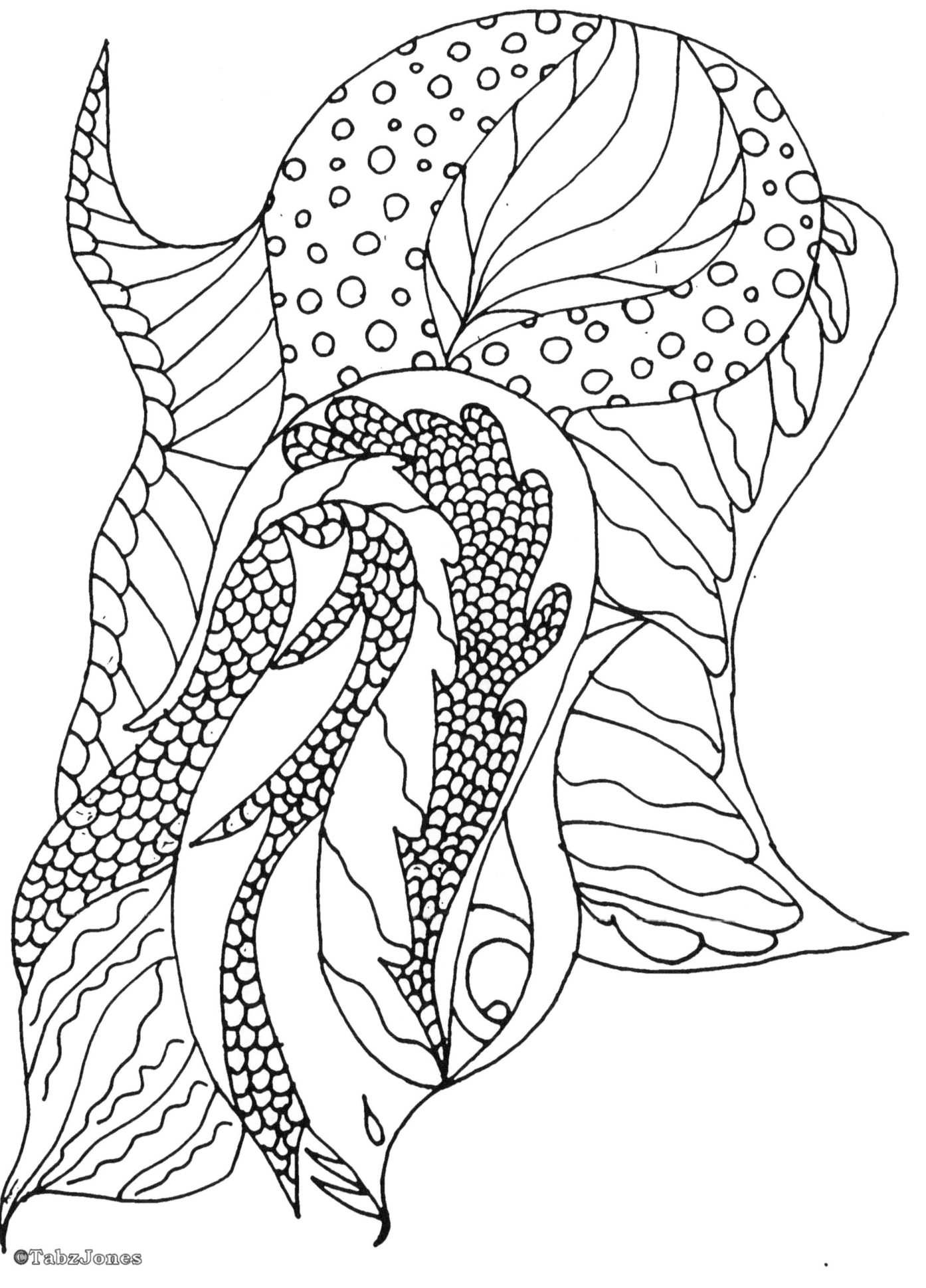
©TabzJones

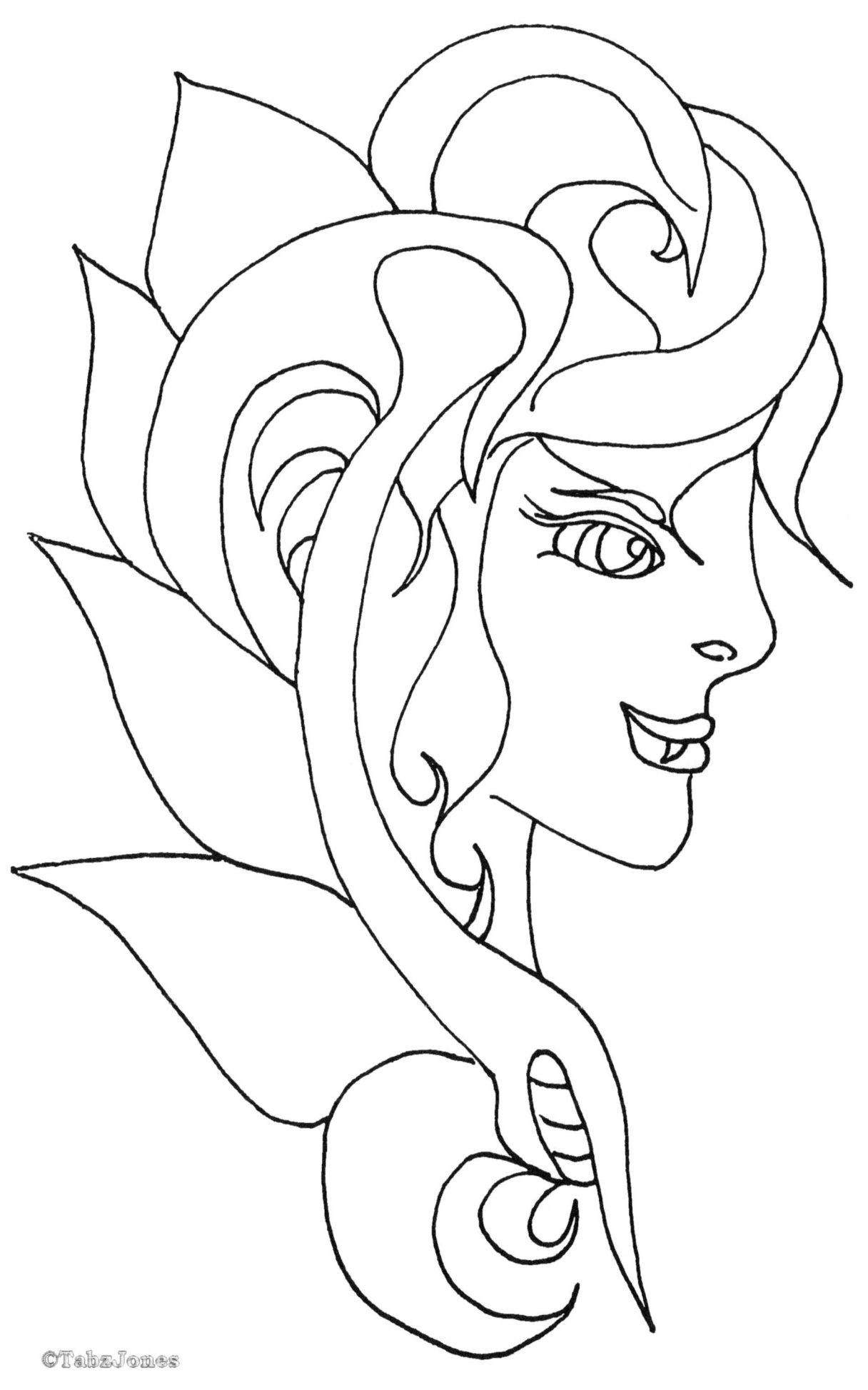

©TabzJones

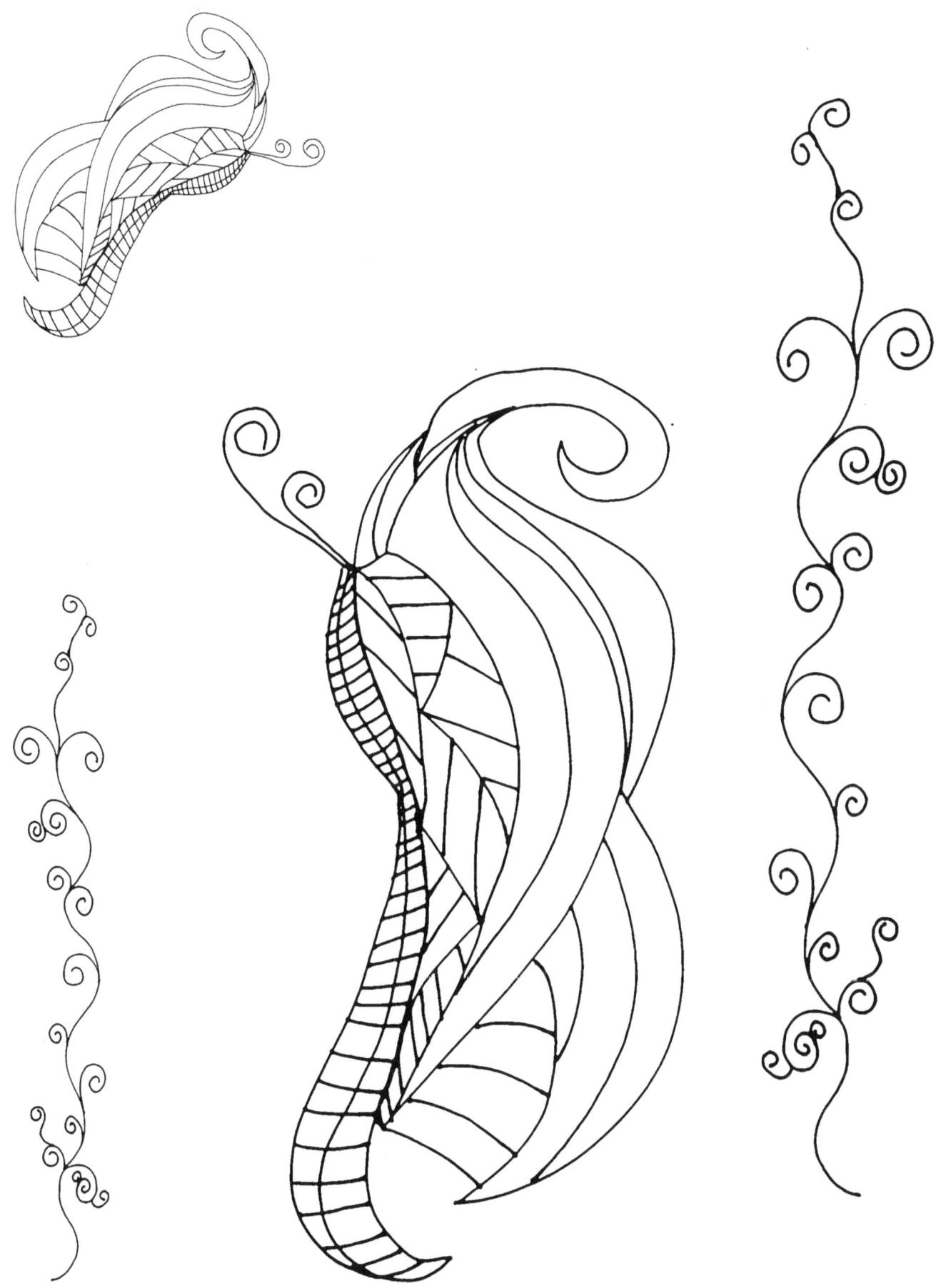

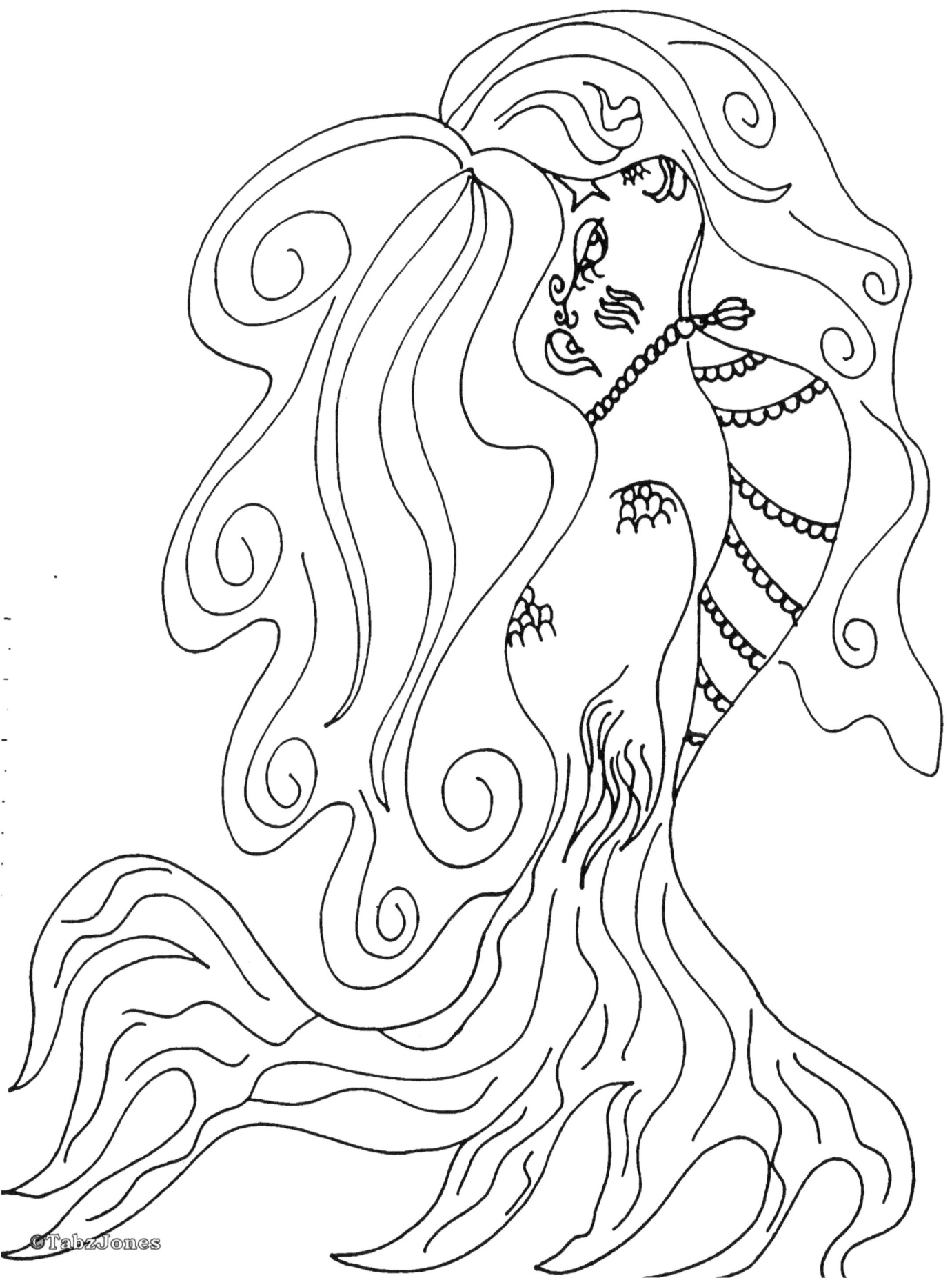

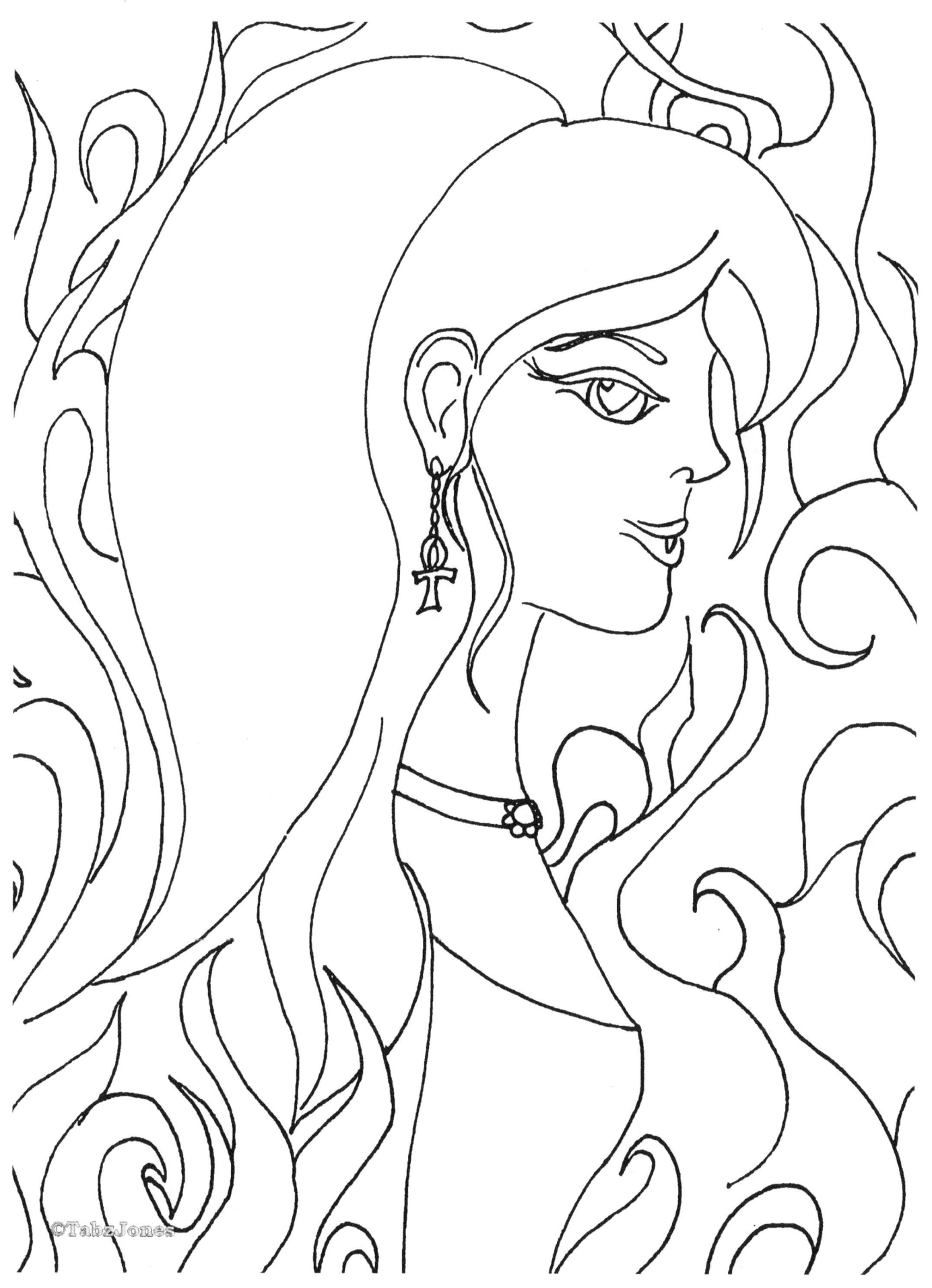

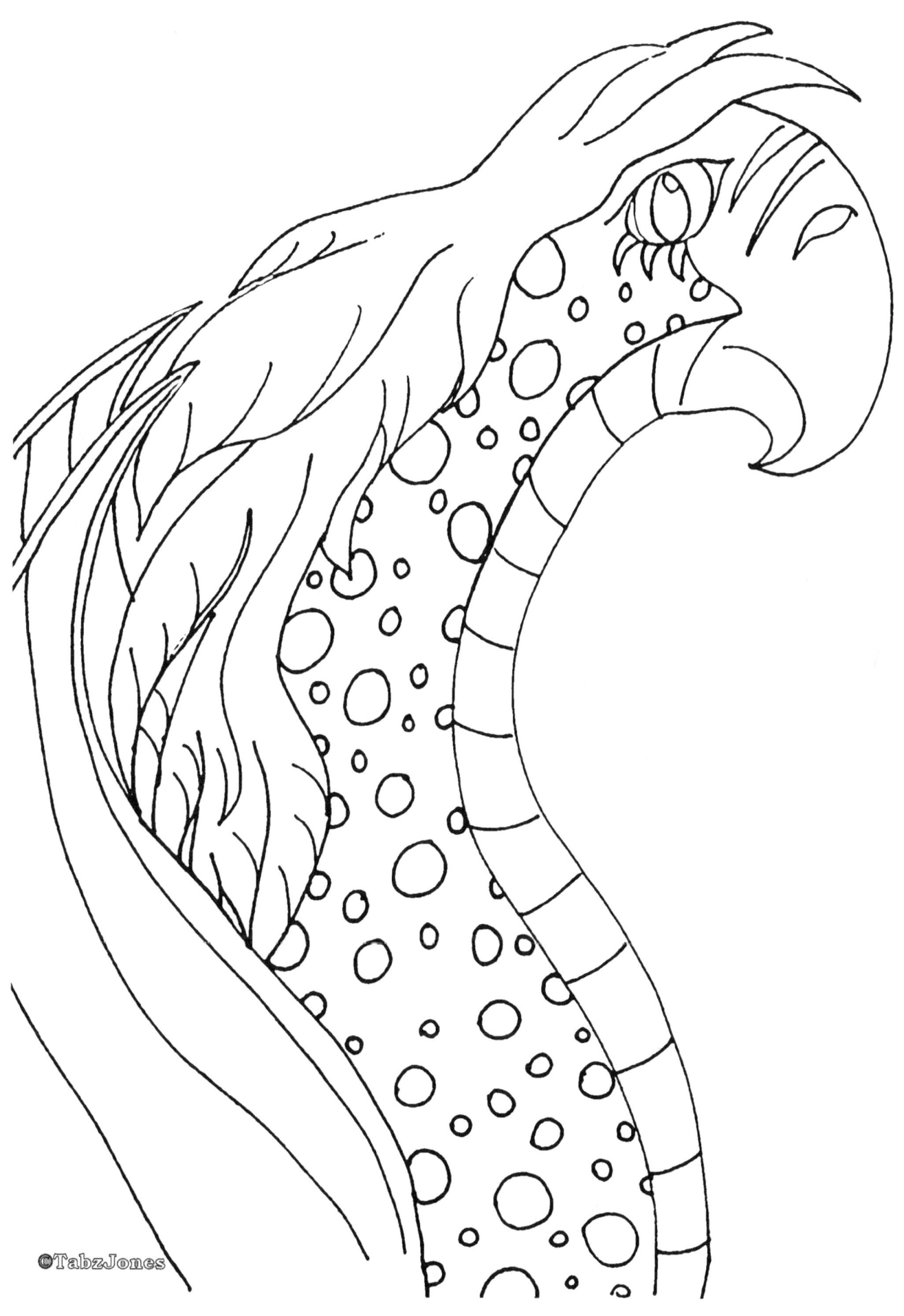

©TabzJones

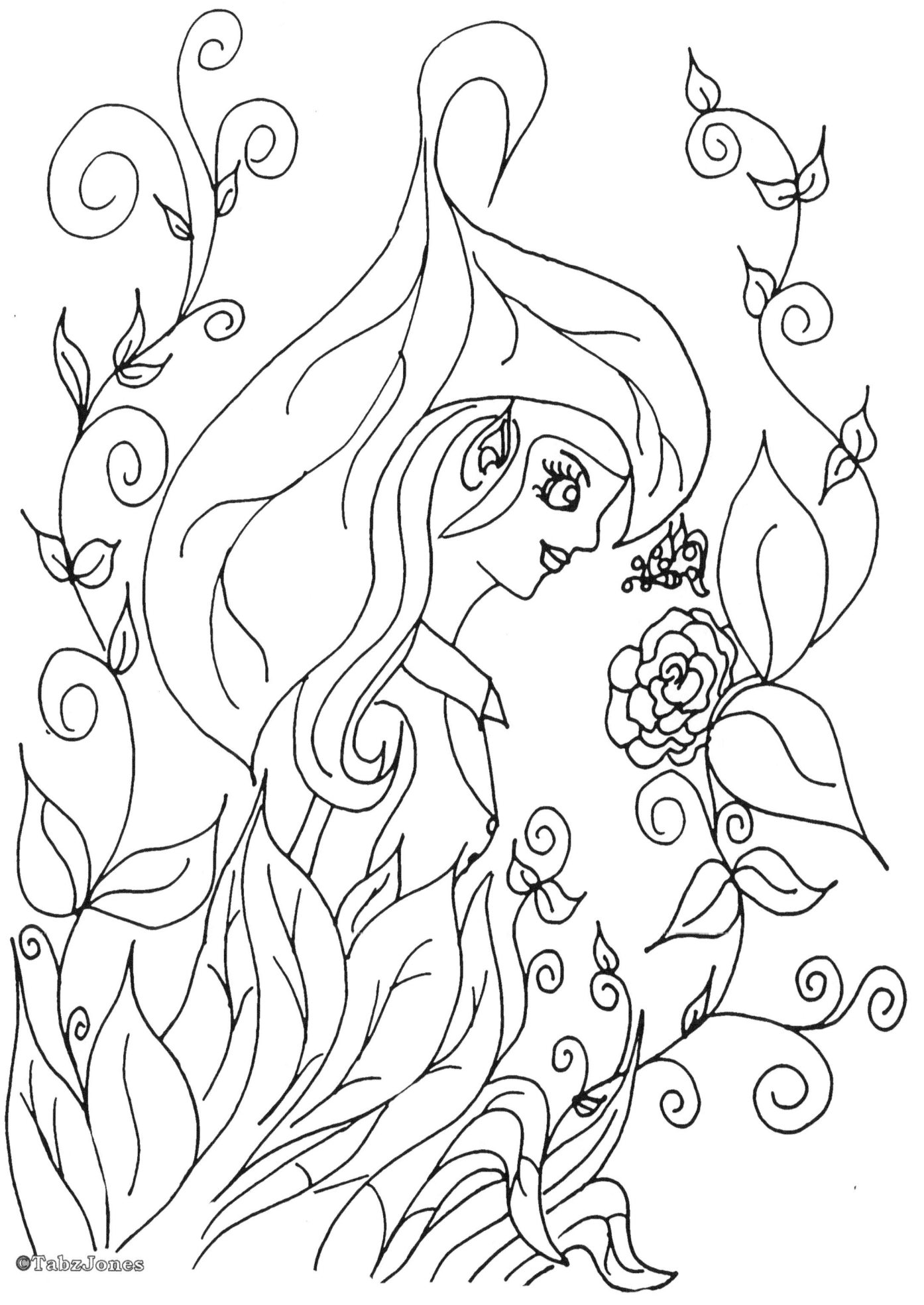
©TabzJones

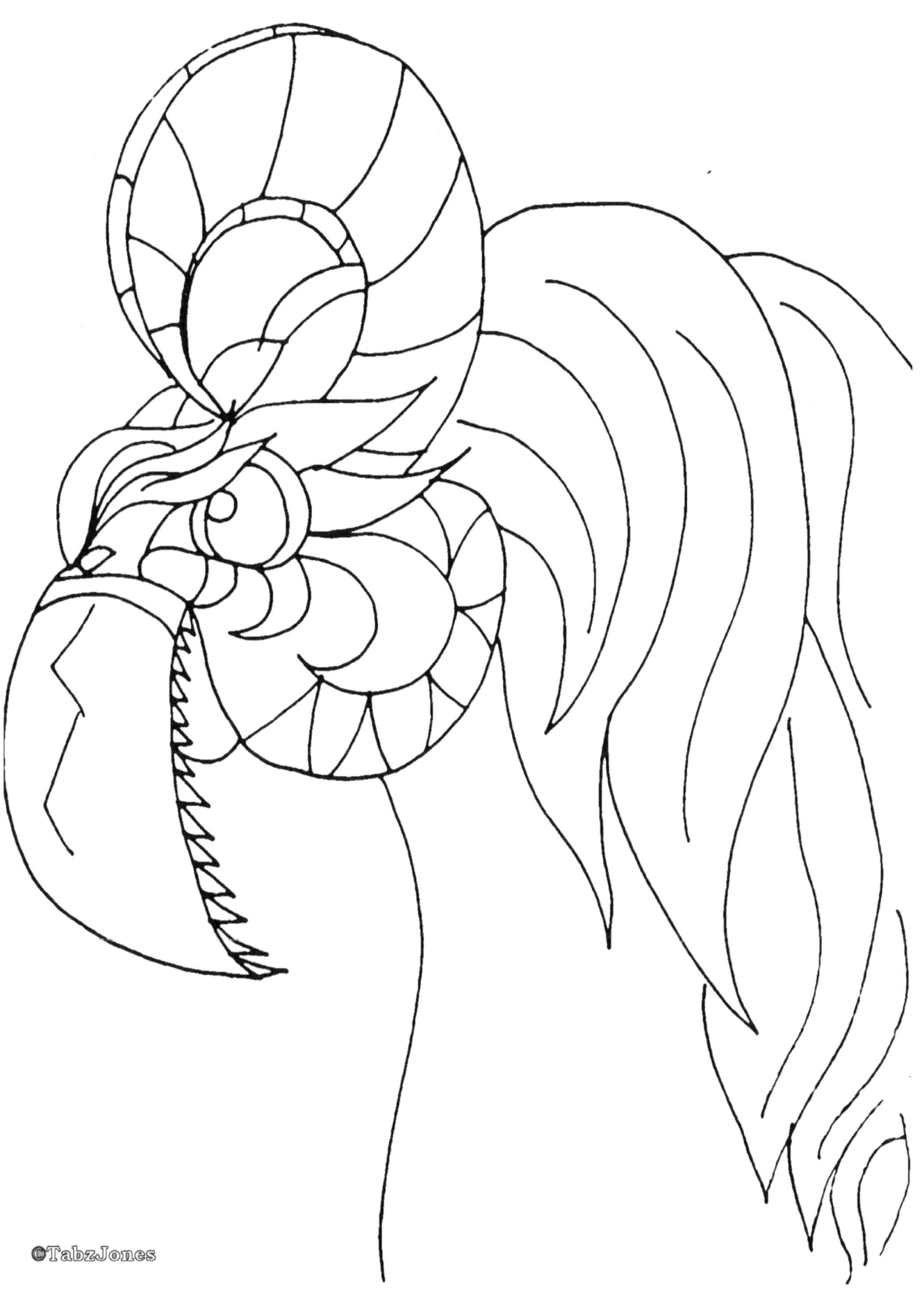

©TabzJones

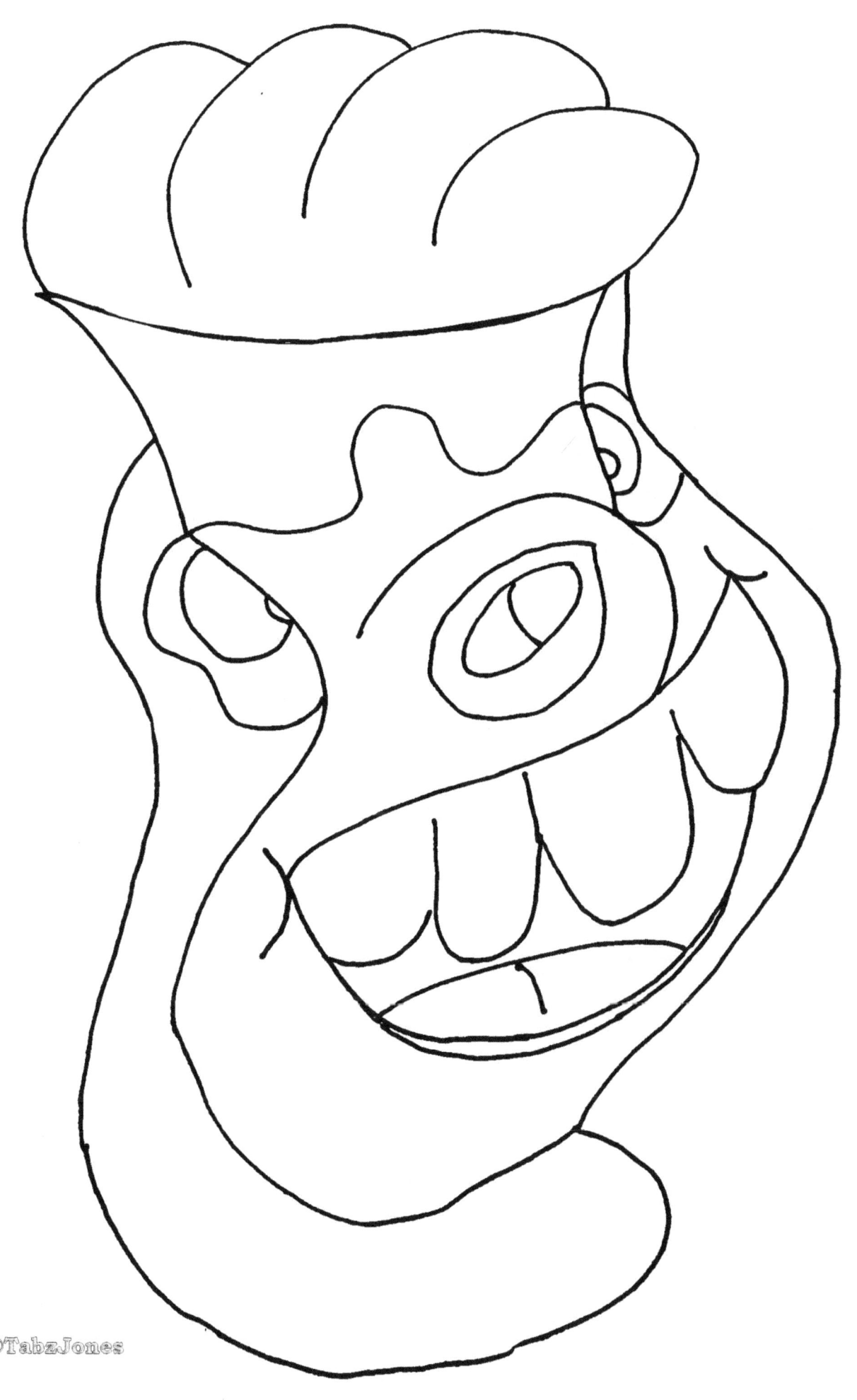

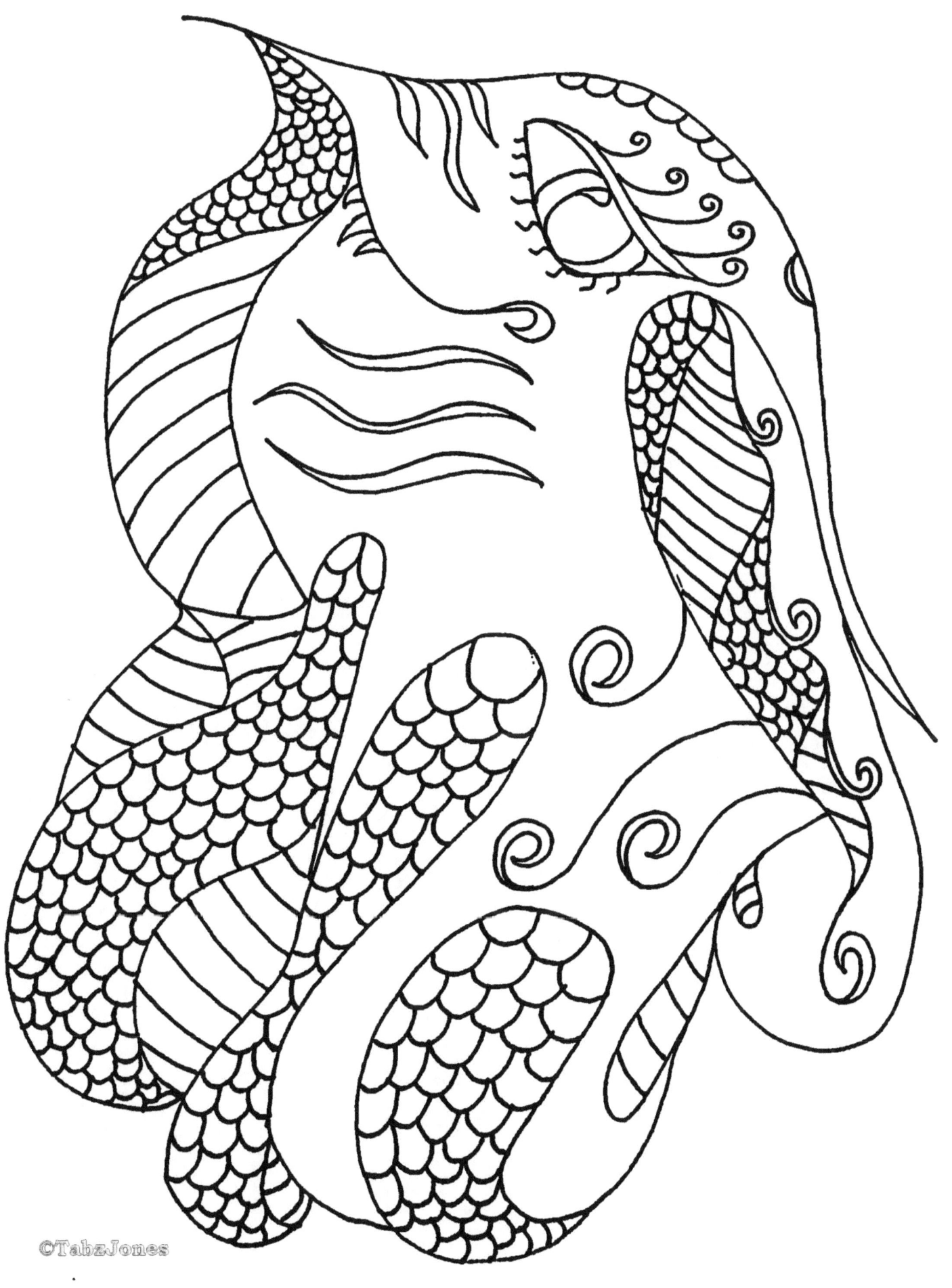

©TabzJones

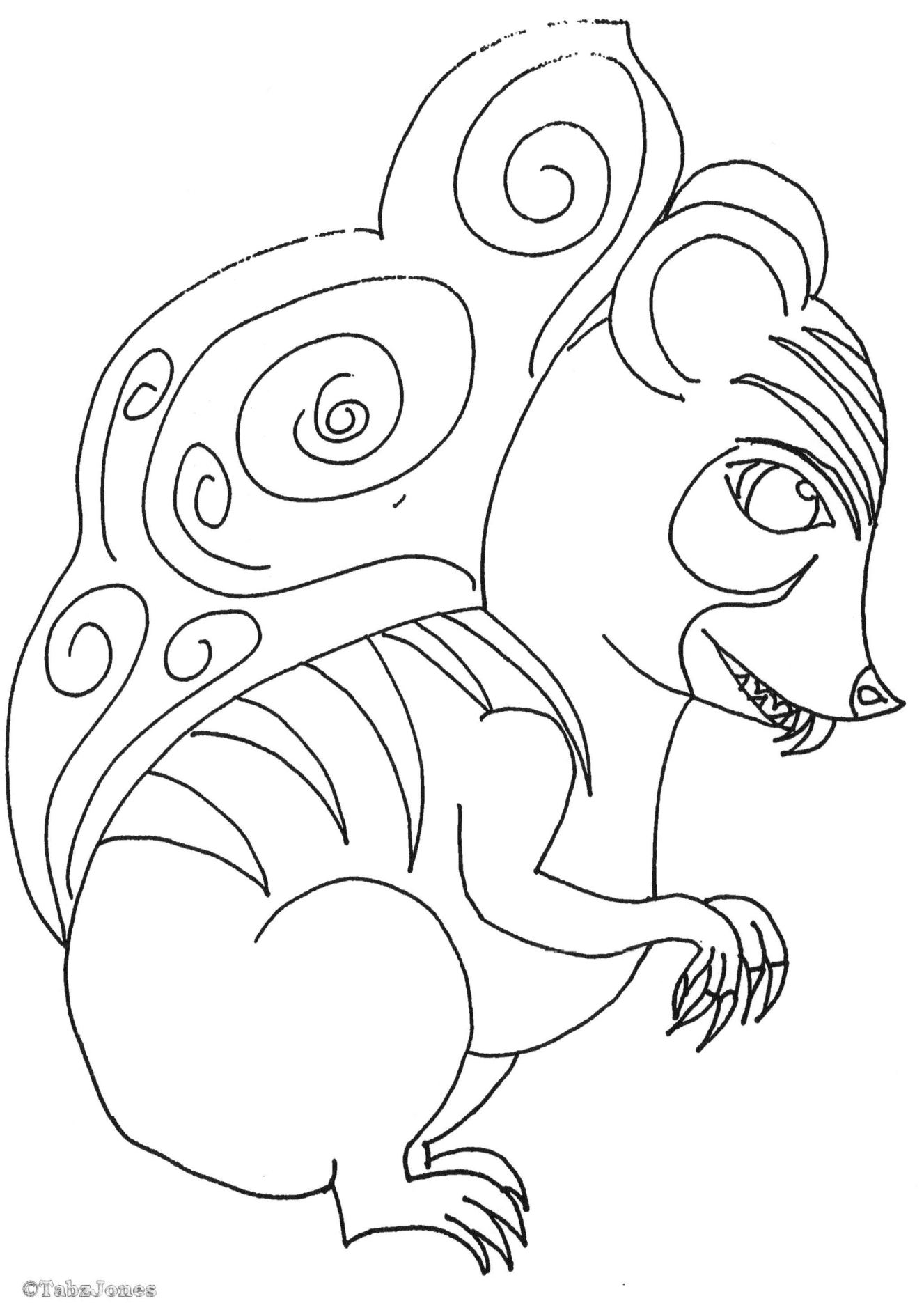

©TabzJones

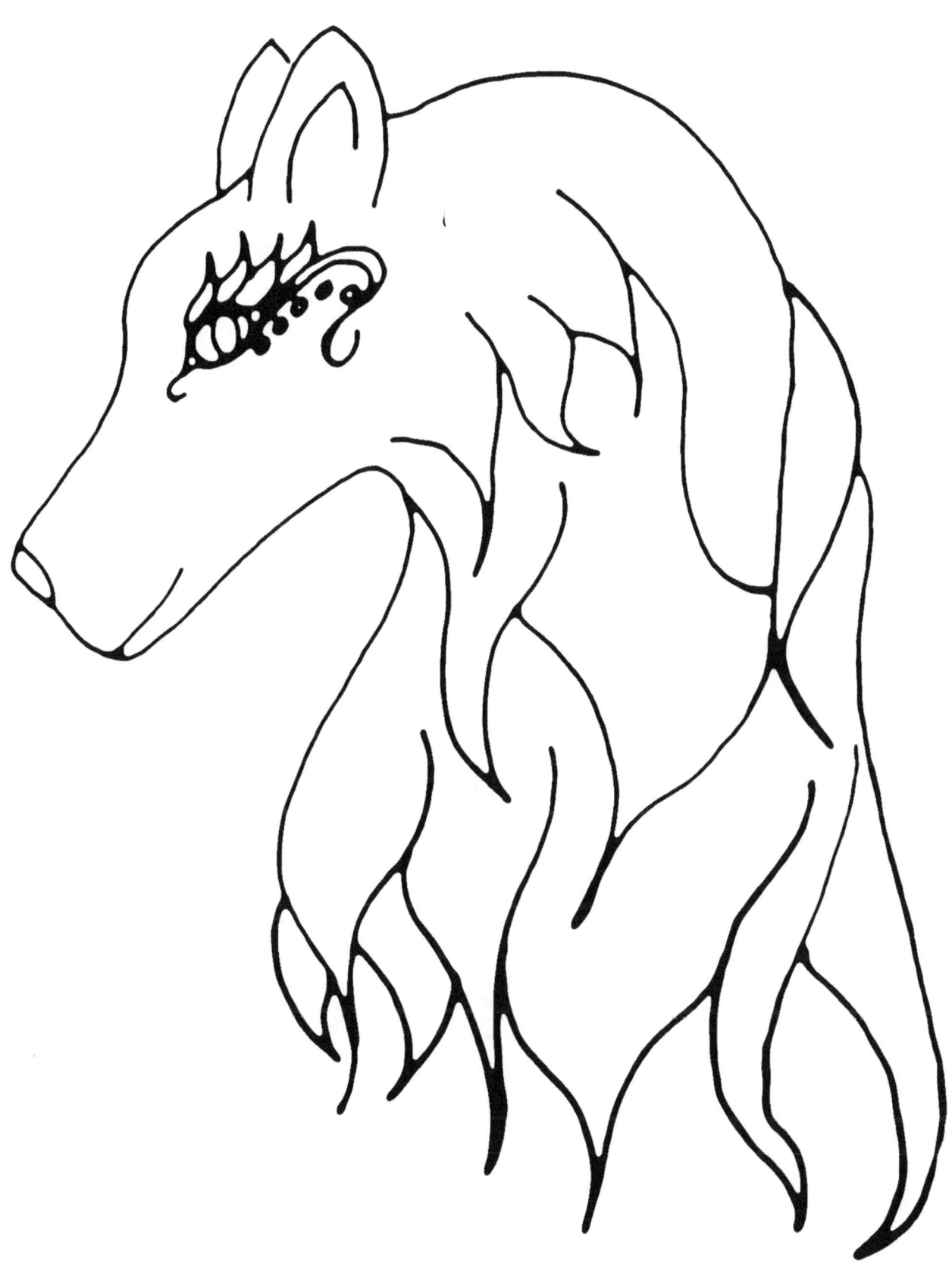

©TabzJones

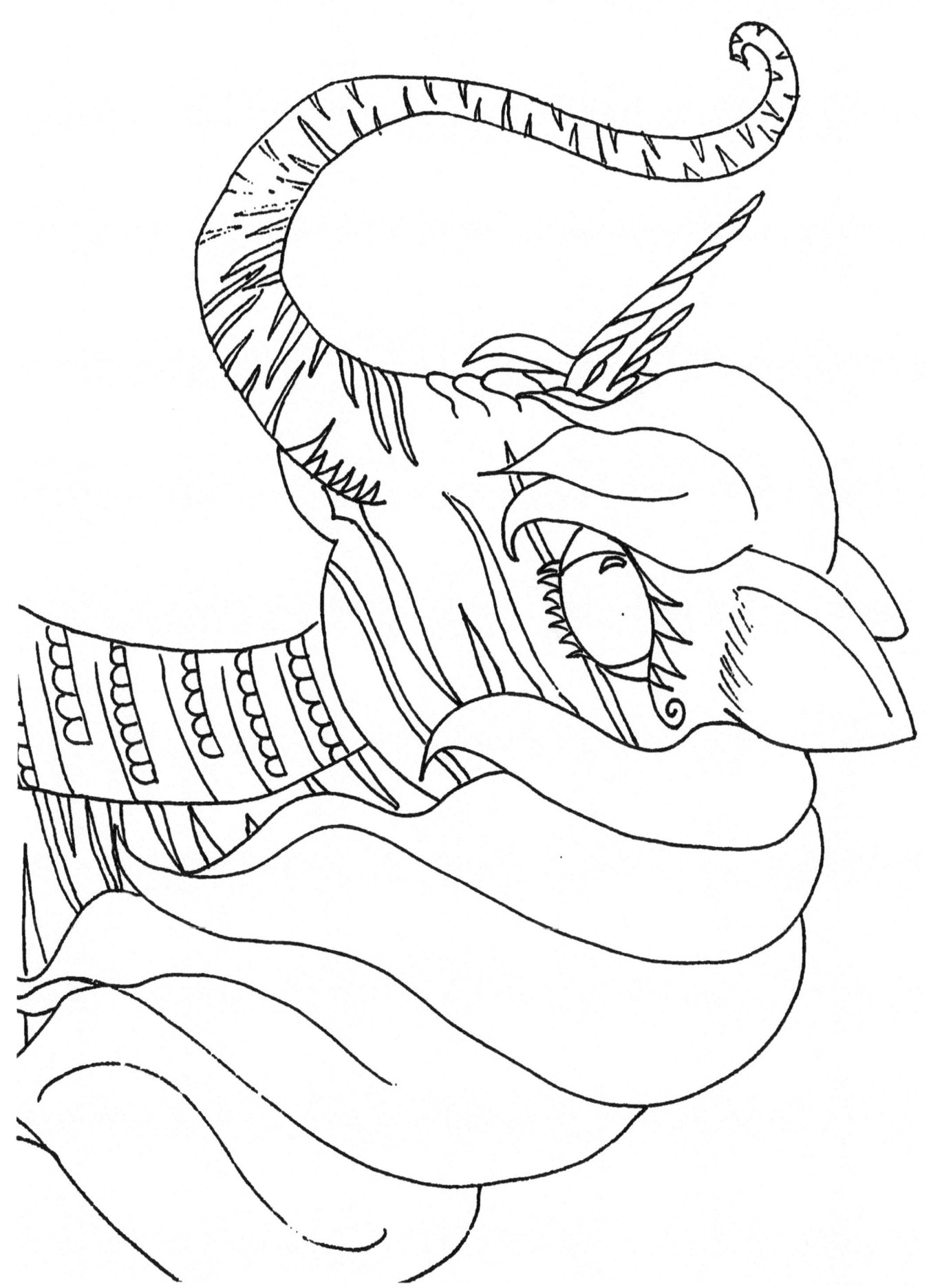

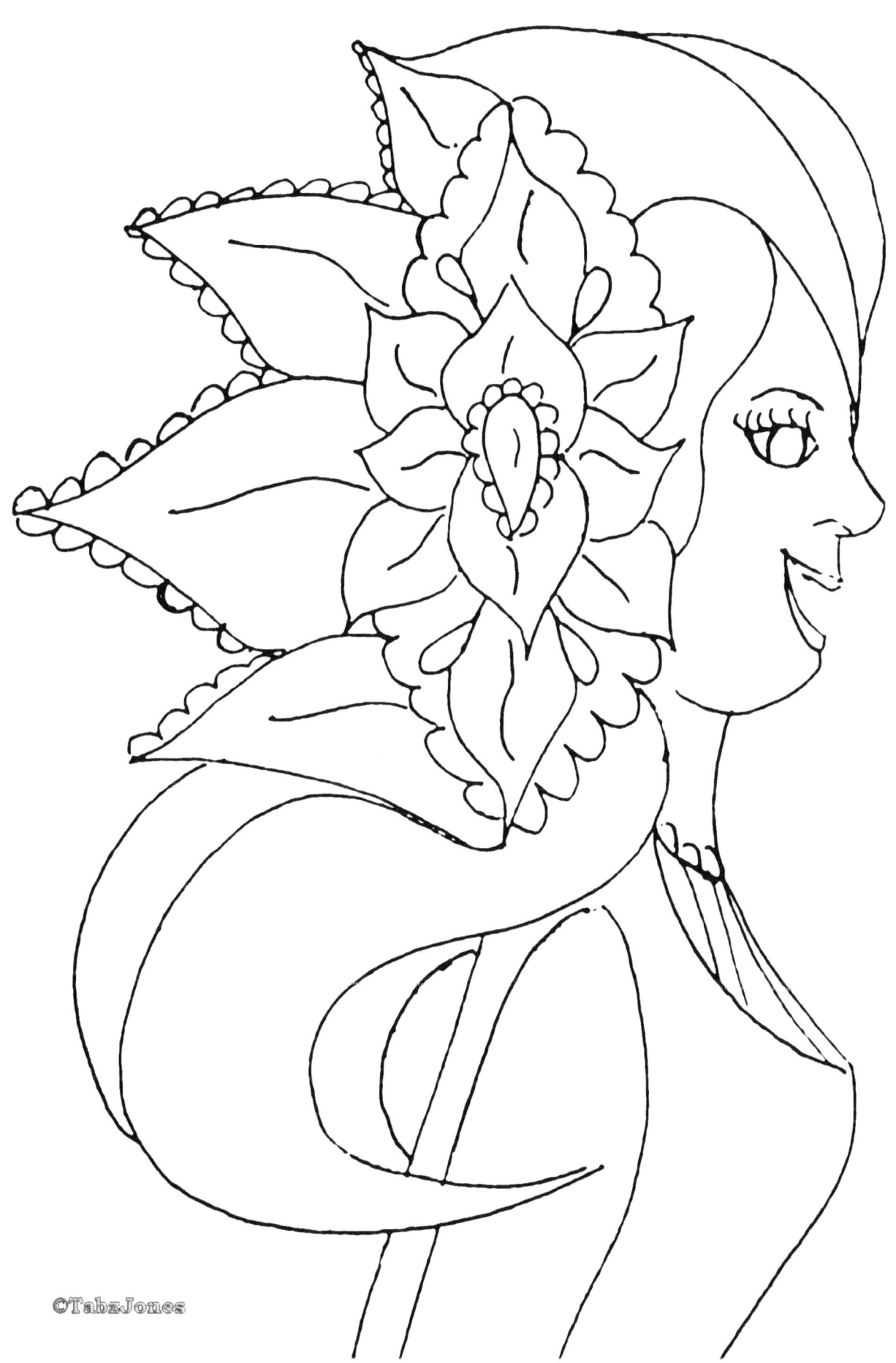

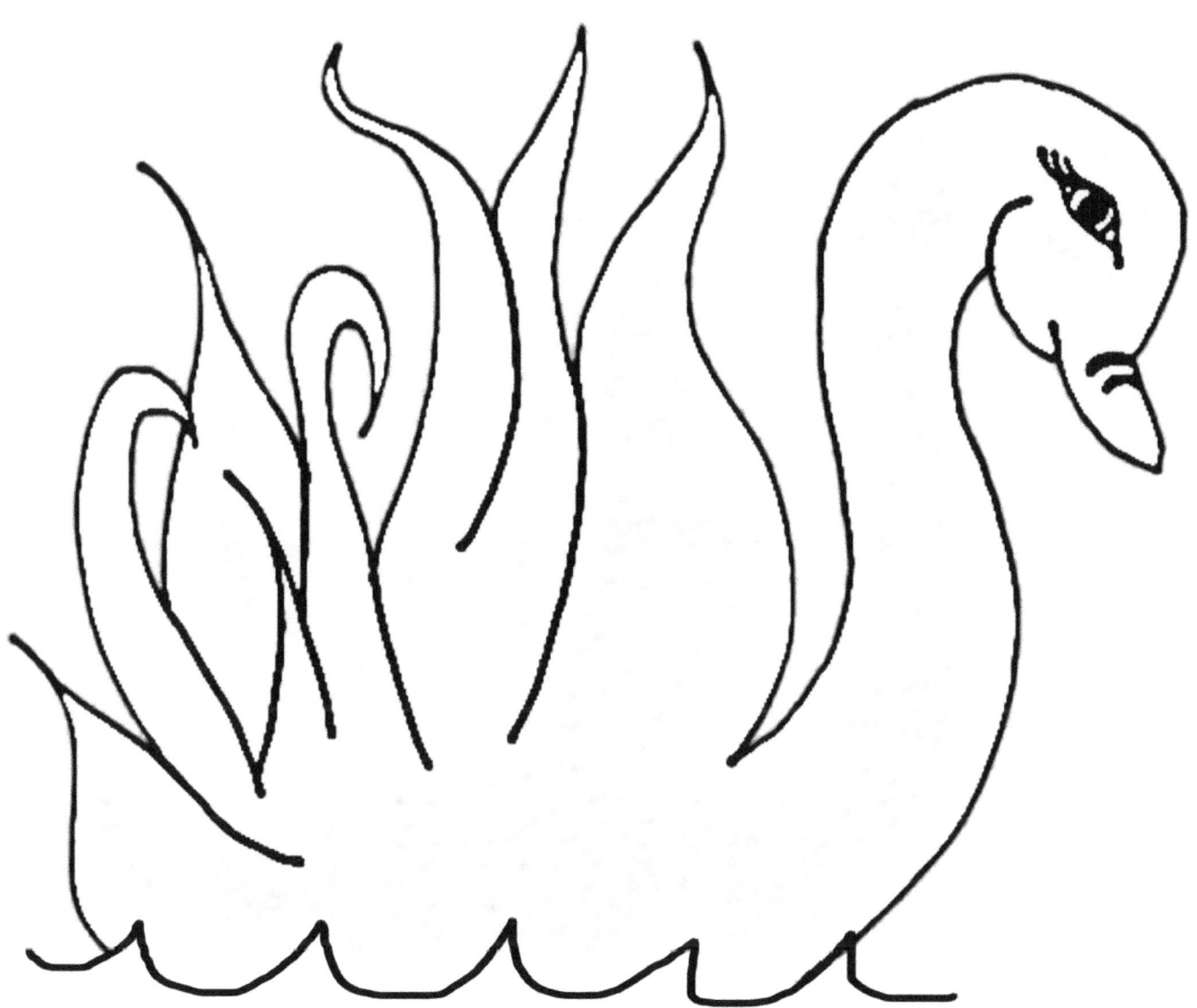

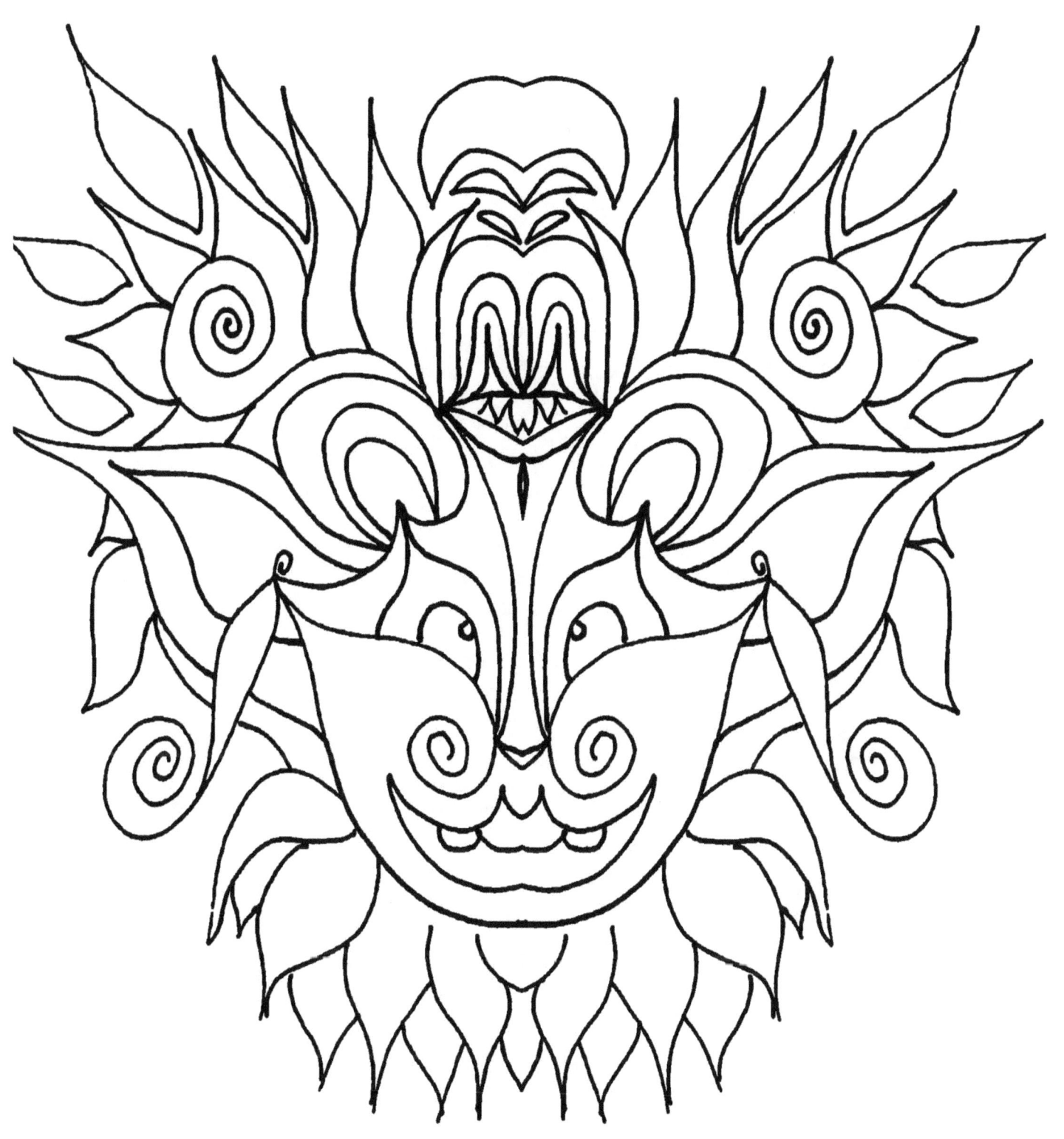

Thank you

for your purchase!

To see the full catalog of my art, don't forget
to stop by
www.gothictoggs.net